MW00875800

The Salad Dressing

Cookbook

Unleash your Creativity with 25 Unique

Salad Dressing Recipes

BY: SOPHIA FREEMAN

COPYRIGHTED

Liability

This publication is meant as an informational tool. The individual purchaser accepts all liability if damages occur because of following the directions or guidelines set out in this publication. The Author bears no responsibility for reparations caused by the misuse or misinterpretation of the content.

Copyright

The content of this publication is solely for entertainment purposes and is meant to be purchased by one individual. Permission is not given to any individual who copies, sells or distributes parts or the whole of this publication unless it is explicitly given by the Author in writing.

My gift to you!

Thank you, cherished reader, for purchasing my book and taking the time to read it. As a special reward for your decision, I would like to offer a gift of free and discounted books directly to your inbox. All you need to do is fill in the box below with your email address and name to start getting amazing offers in the comfort of your own home. You will never miss an offer because a reminder will be sent to you. Never miss a deal and get great deals without having to leave the house! Subscribe now and start saving!

Subscribe to the Newsletter!

Your email address   Subscribe

* * * * ★ ★ ★ ★ ★ * * *

Table of Contents

Unique Salad Dressing Recipes

ZZZZZZZZZZZZZZZZZZZZZZZZZZZZZZZZZZZZZZZZZZZZZZZZZ

1) Sesame and Lime Mayonnaise Dressing

The sesame oil and seeds add a distinctly exotic flavor to this dressing. Using olive oil can be overly harsh and bitter so it is always nice to add different oil with it such as sunflower, sesame, etc.

Makes: 4-6

Total Prep Time: 6 minutes

Ingredient List:

- 1 Tbsp. of sesame seeds
- 1 garlic clove, peeled and finely chopped
- 3 egg yolks
- 4 tsp. of lime juice
- 1 cup of olive oil
- 2 tsp. of sesame oil
- Pinch of sea salt
- Pinch of black pepper

zzzzzzzzzzzzzzzzzzzzzzzzzzzzzzzzzzzzzzzzzzzzzz

Instructions:

Put the sesame seeds, garlic, and sea salt into a small bowl.

Mix everything well until you get a smooth paste.

Add the egg yolks, lime juice, and black pepper.

Using an electric whisk, whisk until the mixture is frothy.

Whisk in the olive oil very gradually, little at the time.

Mix well until it is thickening and glossy.

Whisk in the sesame oil and season to taste if needed.

2) Green Goddess Dressing

Avery popular dressing from the 70s, 80s with the base of a mayonnaise and you just finish it with some sour cream, anchovy, and mixed herbs. Don't hesitate to use some herbs you like and even add some mints if you want a minter flavor to it.

Makes: 4-6

Total Prep Time: 5 minutes

Ingredient List:

- 2 eggs yolk
- 2 tsp. of white vinegar
- 1 cup of sunflower oil
- 1 tsp. of Dijon mustard
- 4 anchovy filets, chopped
- 1 garlic clove, finely chopped
- ¼ cup of sour cream
- ¼ cup of fresh mixed herbs, parsley, tarragon, chive, etc.
- Salt and pepper

zzz

Instructions:

Place the eggs yolk and the white vinegar into a food processor or blender.

Add the mustard and season.

Process for 15 seconds or until blended.

Add the sunflower oil in a thin steady stream slowly and whisk in the same time.

Blend everything until the mixture is thick and creamy.

Add the anchovy, garlic, sour cream, and the mixed herbs.

Blend everything again until you get a smooth, creamy mixture.

3) Blue Cheese Vinaigrette

This tasty blue cheese dressing will go well with any green salad and is perfect as well, if you add some apples and pears with a grilled steak for example. Try to use a good quality blue cheese and with a strong flavor and don't hesitate to add more to the dressing depending on your taste.

Makes: 4-6

Total Prep Time: 10 minutes

Ingredient List:

- ½ cup of blue cheese, crumble
- 2 Tbsp. of caster sugar
- 2 Tbsp. of red wine vinegar
- 4 Tbsp. of olive oil
- Pinch of salt
- Pinch of ground pepper

ZZZZZZZZZZZZZZZZZZZZZZZZZZZZZZZZZZZZZZZZZZZZZZZZ

Instructions:

Combine the sugar and the red wine vinegar together.

Whisk well until the sugar is completely dissolved.

Add the olive oil in a thin steady stream slowly and whisk in the same time.

Add the salt and ground pepper and whisk again.

Add and stir the blue cheese into the vinaigrette and mix it gently.

4) Yogurt & lemon and Grapefruit Dressing

This tangy lemon and grapefruit yogurt dressing with a touch of ginger will be perfect for any fish salad you are preparing. Salads are not always just leaves but can be a mixture of other ingredients with it.

Makes: 4

Total Prep Time: 5 minutes

Ingredient List:

- 1 lemon, juice
- 1 cup of yogurt
- 2 Tbsp. of olive oil
- 3 Tbsp. of grapefruit juice
- 1 tsp. of mustard
- Pinch of ginger
- 1 Tbsp. of chive, chopped

ZZZZZZZZZZZZZZZZZZZZZZZZZZZZZZZZZZZZZZZZZZZZZZ

Instructions:

Combine the yogurt with the olive oil in a large bowl.

Add the lemon juice and grapefruit juice.

Mix everything well and add the mustard.

Add the ginger and the chive.

Mix everything well and place in the fridge for 20 minutes before using it.

5) Caesar Dressing

One of the most famous salad dressings is created by an Italian immigrant Caesar Cardini who lived in Mexico in 1924. After he moved to L.A. where he began to bottle and sells the famous Caesar dressing. Today you can find so many variations from the original recipe but this one is my favorite.

Makes: 4-6

Total Prep Time: 10 minutes

Ingredient List:

- 1 egg yolk
- 1 garlic, crushed
- 2 anchovy filets in oil, drained and chopped
- 1 Tbsp. of lemon juice
- 1 tsp. of Worcestershire sauce
- ½ cup of olive oil
- 1 ½ Tbsp. of grated Parmesan
- Salt and pepper

zzzzzzzzzzzzzzzzzzzzzzzzzzzzzzzzzzzzzzzzzzzzzzzzz

Instructions:

Whisk the egg yolk in a small bowl.

Add the garlic, anchovies, lemon juice, Worcestershire sauce and season.

Whisk again with all the ingredients together.

Gradually whisk in the olive oil a little at a time until thick and glossy.

Add 2 Tbsp. of water to thin the dressing.

Stir in the parmesan and mix with the salad.

6) Vinaigrette

The famous classic French vinaigrette recipe and without any hesitation it will go well with any salad of your choice, simple and easy to make. It is important to combine the salt and vinegar together first, since it will allow the salt to dissolve itself in it.

Makes: 4

Total Prep Time: 5 minutes

Ingredient List:

- 1 Tbsp. of vinegar
- 3 Tbsp. of oil
- Pinch of salt
- Pinch of ground pepper

zzzzzzzzzzzzzzzzzzzzzzzzzzzzzzzzzzzzzzzzzzzzz

Instructions:

Dissolve the salt with the vinegar in a large bowl.

Pour the oil in a thin stream.

Add the oil slowly in a thin steady stream and whisk in the same time.

Make sure everything is well emulsified.

Add some ground pepper.

Whisk the vinaigrette again and mix with the salad.

7) Chili Caramel Dressing

The palm sugar, fish sauce, and lime juice in this dressing are providing that deliciously sweet, salty, sour flavors so typical for Southeast Asian cuisine. The heat from the chili makes this dressing perfect to accompaniment any salad with grilled meats or even grilled fish.

Makes: 4-6

Total Prep Time: 10 minutes

Ingredient List:

- ½ cup of peanut oil
- 2 red chilies, deseeded and thinly sliced
- 2 garlic cloves, peeled and finely chopped
- 1 tsp. of grated ginger
- 4 Tbsp. of palm sugar
- 2 Tbsp. of fish sauce
- 1 lime, juice

zzzzzzzzzzzzzzzzzzzzzzzzzzzzzzzzzzzzzzzzzzzzzzz

Instructions:

Heat the peanut oil into a small saucepan.

Add the chilies, garlic, and ginger and heat gently for 3 minutes.

Add the palm sugar, 3 Tbsp. of water, and the fish sauce.

Add the lime juice and heat gently until the sugar has dissolved.

Increase the heat and simmer for 5 minutes.

When the mixture is syrupy, stop the heat

Set aside and let it cool off before using it.

8) Thousand Island Dressing

The Thousand Island dressing is a continuation of the mayonnaise by adding more ingredients to it but remember not to make it too liquid. It is always the best to make the mayonnaise first and add the other ingredients after. You can as well put some garlic too.

Makes: 4-6

Total Prep Time: 5 minutes

Ingredient List:

- 2 eggs yolk
- 2 tsp. of white vinegar
- 1 cup of sunflower oil
- 1 tsp. of Dijon mustard
- 2 tsp. of tomato purée
- Pinch of cayenne
- 1 Tbsp. of celery, finely chopped
- 1 Tbsp. of sweet pickle, chopped
- 1 tsp. of capers, chopped
- 2 tsp. of Worcestershire sauce
- Salt and pepper

ZZ

Instructions:

Place the eggs yolk and the white vinegar into a food processor or blender.

Add the mustard and season.

Process for 15 seconds or until blended.

Add the sunflower oil in a thin steady stream slowly and whisk in the same time.

Blend everything until the mixture is thick and creamy.

Add the tomato purée, Cayenne pepper, and Worcestershire sauce.

Add the pickle, capers, and celery.

Blend everything again until you get a creamy smooth mixture.

9) Coconut & Wasabi Vinaigrette

The exotic taste of the coconut and the flavor of the wasabi from Japan will bring a very interesting and unusual dressing to your salad. Don't hesitate to add more oil or coconut or even wasabi to your liking. A vinaigrette should be done the way you like.

Makes: 4

Total Prep Time: 4 minutes

Ingredient List:

- 2 Tbsp. of olive oil
- 1 Tbsp. of grated coconut
- 3 Tbsp. of coconut milk
- 1 tsp. of wasabi paste
- 1 tsp. of lemon juice
- Salt and pepper

zzzzzzzzzzzzzzzzzzzzzzzzzzzzzzzzzzzzzzzzzzzzz

Instructions:

Combine the coconut milk and the lemon juice in a small bowl.

Add and whisk the wasabi paste and the grated coconut.

Add a pinch of salt and whisk again.

Add the olive oil slowly in a thin steady stream and whisk in the same time.

Add some pepper and whisk well again.

10) Tartar Dressing

The tartar sauce-dressing is a mayonnaise base to which you add other ingredients to make it. It is very suitable for fried or grilled fish and can be uses either as a sauce or as a dressing. Don't forget to keep it in the fridge.

Makes: 4-6

Total Prep Time: 8 minutes

Ingredient List:

- 2 eggs yolk
- 2 tsp. of white vinegar
- 1 cup of sunflower oil
- 1 tsp. of Dijon mustard
- 4 Tbsp. of capers, finely chopped
- 6 Tbsp. of gherkins, finely chopped
- 2 Tbsp. of fresh parsley, finely chopped
- 2 Tbsp. of double cream
- Salt and pepper

zzzzzzzzzzzzzzzzzzzzzzzzzzzzzzzzzzzzzzzzzzzzz

Instructions:

Place the eggs yolk and the white vinegar into a food processor or blender.

Add the mustard and season.

Process for 15 seconds or until blended.

Add the sunflower oil in a thin steady stream slowly and whisk in the same time.

Blend everything until the mixture is thick and creamy.

Add the capers, parsley, and gherkins and whisk well.

Pour the double cream and whisk well again.

Adjust the seasoning and add if needed.

11) Coffee Dressing

This is for the coffee lover, something different but, I am sure, will be a winner for some people. Depending on how strong you like it just add more grounded coffee or not. This dressing will go well with endives. Obviously try not to abuse it but doctors say that coffee is good for health.

Makes: 4

Total Prep Time: 5 minutes

Ingredient List:

- 1 Tbsp. of ground coffee
- 2 shallots, finely chopped
- 1 tsp. of sugar
- 1 Tbsp. of balsamic vinegar
- 1/3 cup of sunflower oil
- Salt and pepper

zzzzzzzzzzzzzzzzzzzzzzzzzzzzzzzzzzzzzzzzzzzzzz

Instructions:

In a small bowl combine the balsamic vinegar with the ground coffee.

Add the sugar and season well.

Whisk everything until the ground coffee and sugar are dissolved.

Add the shallots and whisk again.

Very gradually whisk in the sunflower oil, little at the time.

Serve immediately when ready.

12) Tahini & Garlic Yoghurt Dressing

Tahini is made from ground sesame seeds and is largely used in eastern Mediterranean and Middle Eastern cooking. Here it helps to flavor the yoghurt and results in a great accompaniment to all your salads but as well to any roasted vegetables or even some grilled lamb.

Makes: 4

Total Prep Time: 35 minutes

Ingredient List:

- 1 cup of Greek yoghurt
- 1 garlic clove, crushed
- 1 ½ Tbsp. of tahini
- 1 Tbsp. of lemon juice
- Salt and pepper

zzzzzzzzzzzzzzzzzzzzzzzzzzzzzzzzzzzzzzzzzzzzzzzzz

Instructions:

Combine the yoghurt and the garlic in a large bowl.

Add the tahini and the lemon juice.

Season and mix everything well.

Cover and set aside to infuse for 30 minutes.

Mix with the salad and enjoy.

13) Curry Dressing

This curry dressing will be perfect for any hot and spicy salad you are going to make. Don't hesitate to use different spices or paste while making your dressing - all depends on your choice.

Makes: 4

Total Prep Time: 4 minutes

Ingredient List:

- 2 Tbsp. of vinegar
- 6 Tbsp. of sunflower oil
- 1 tsp. of ground ginger
- 1 tsp. of curry powder
- 1 tsp. of ground cumin
- Pinch of salt

ZZZZZZZZZZZZZZZZZZZZZZZZZZZZZZZZZZZZZZZZZZZZ

Instructions:

Dissolve the salt into the vinegar in a small bowl.

Add the ground ginger, the cumin and the curry powder.

Mix everything well.

Add the sunflower oil in a thin steady stream slowly.

Whisk in the same time until you have used all the oil.

14) Strawberries Vinaigrette

This colorful and fruity vinaigrette made from strawberries will be great with any leaves you will decide to mix. So easy to make and you can use other fruit such as raspberry, berries, etc. if you want it to be sweeter replace the salt with sugar.

Makes: 4-6

Total Prep Time: 10 minutes

Ingredient List:

- 1 cup of fresh strawberries
- ½ cup of cider vinegar
- 4 Tbsp. of sunflower oil
- Pinch of salt
- Pinch of ground pepper

zzzzzzzzzzzzzzzzzzzzzzzzzzzzzzzzzzzzzzzzzzzzzzzz

Instructions:

Cup the strawberries into small pieces.

Combine the vinegar with the strawberries in a small bowl.

Cover and leave in the fridge for few hours.

Blend the strawberries vinegar until smooth.

Add the salt and whisk well to dissolve it.

Add the sunflower oil slowly in a thin steady stream and whisk in the same time.

Add the pepper and whisk well again.

15) Green Tea Dressing

A preparation of highly original dressing is perfect to accompany any poached fish with all your greens salad without forgetting a nice cup of green tea. If you cannot find some green tea powder, use a green tea bag with three tsp. of water.

Makes: 4

Total Prep Time: 4 minutes

Ingredient List:

- 3 tsp. of green tea powder
- 2 Tbsp. of sunflower oil
- 1 tsp. of white vinegar
- 1 tsp. of rice vinegar
- 1 Tbsp. of mustard
- Pinch of salt
- Pinch of ground black pepper

ZZZZZZZZZZZZZZZZZZZZZZZZZZZZZZZZZZZZZZZZZZZZZZ

Instructions:

Combine the mustard with the salt and the black pepper in a small bowl.

Add the green tea powder and mix everything.

Add and whisk in the white vinegar.

Add and whisk in the rice vinegar.

Add the sunflower oil slowly in a thin steady stream and whisk in the same time.

Toss the dressing with your salad and enjoy.

16) Spicy Peanut Butter Dressing

This spicy peanut butter dressing can be served with any salad of your choice but it needs to be prepared in advance. You should leave it in the fridge to chill down a day before you require using it. Just shake it well before and toss it to your salad and enjoy.

Makes: 4

Total Prep Time: 5 minutes

Ingredient List:

- 6 Tbsp. of crunchy peanut butter
- 6 Tbsp. of olive oil
- 2 Tbsp. of soy sauce
- 1 red chili, seeded and finely chopped
- 2 Tbsp. of sesame oil
- 4 tsp. of lime juice

zzzzzzzzzzzzzzzzzzzzzzzzzzzzzzzzzzzzzzzzzzzzzzzzz

Instructions:

Put the peanut butter in a small mixing bowl.

Gradually whisk in the olive oil.

Then gradually whisk the soy sauce.

Add and stir in the chopped red chili.

Add and stir in the sesame oil and lime juice.

Mix everything until well combined.

17) Honey and Ginger Vinaigrette

A delicious honey vinaigrette with the flavor of ginger which will go well on your salad with some nice grilled duck or some other grilled meat you will decide to do on the barbecue. You can add as well some parsley into the vinaigrette.

Makes: 4-6

Total Prep Time: 6 minutes

Ingredient List:

- 2 Tbsp. of honey
- 1 tsp. of ground ginger
- 1 garlic clove, finely chopped
- 2 shallots, finely chopped
- 3 Tbsp. of olive oil
- 1 Tbsp. of soy sauce
- 1 Tbsp. of water
- 1 Tbsp. of lemon juice
- Salt and pepper

ZZ

Instructions:

Combine the olive oil and the honey together in a small bowl.

Add the soy sauce and the water.

Whisk everything well and season.

Add and whisk the lemon juice.

Add the ground ginger, garlic, and shallots.

Whisk everything well and toss with the salad.

18) Sesame and Orange Dressing

Orange and sesame go absolutely great together. Presence of the fruit does bring some freshness to the dressing and to the salad. Add some seeds to give the extra crunchiness to it. Don't hesitate to add some hazelnut too.

Makes: 4

Total Prep Time: 4 minutes

Ingredient List:

- 1 orange, juice
- 1 Tbsp. of sesame seeds, toasted
- 1 Tbsp. of honey
- 1 Tbsp. of sesame oil
- 1 Tbsp. of hazelnut oil

ZZZZZZZZZZZZZZZZZZZZZZZZZZZZZZZZZZZZZZZZZZZ

Instructions:

Combine the sesame oil with the hazelnut oil in a large bowl.

Add the orange juice and the honey.

Whisk everything together.

Add the sesame seeds and whisk again.

Pour to the salad and mix well.

19) Hot Fish and Lime Dressing

This hot fish and lime dressing will go very well with any salad and meat together. You can reduce taste and adjust its piquancy and if needed add more lime juice or fish sauce to reduce its sharpness.

Makes: 4

Total Prep Time: 5 minutes

Ingredient List:

- 3 Tbsp. of fish sauce
- 1 ½ Tbsp. of lime juice
- 2 garlic clove, crushed
- 1 red chili, seeded and very finely chopped
- 1 green chili, seeded and very finely chopped
- 1 tsp. of demerara sugar

zzzzzzzzzzzzzzzzzzzzzzzzzzzzzzzzzzzzzzzzzzzzzz

Instructions:

Heat the fish sauce into a small sauce pan.

Add the garlic and lemon juice.

Add the green and red chili and the sugar.

Heat everything gently and stir constantly.

Let it reduce for 2 to 3 minutes.

Stop the heat and let it set aside.

When it is cool down to room temperature mix it with the salad.

20) Ravigote Dressing

This classic French dressing recipe will go well with any salad of your choice. You can even serve it with some cold meat such as beef. The selection of mixed herbs is really up to you, you can always put some parsley, thyme, basil, rosemary, etc.

Makes: 4

Total Prep Time: 10 minutes

Ingredient List:

- 2 Tbsp. of vinegar
- 6 Tbsp. of sunflower oil
- 2 small shallots, finely chopped
- 1 Tbsp. of caper, finely chopped
- 1 Tbsp. of mix herbs, finely chopped
- Pinch of salt
- Pinch of ground pepper

zzzzzzzzzzzzzzzzzzzzzzzzzzzzzzzzzzzzzzzzzzzzzzzz

Instructions:

Dissolve the salt with the vinegar in a large bowl.

Pour the oil in a thin stream.

Add the sunflower oil slowly in a thin steady stream and whisk in the same time.

Add some ground pepper and whisk again.

Add the shallots, capers and mix herbs.

Whisk well again.

Leave the dressing to rest for 30 minutes and mix with the salad.

21) Japanese Soy & Wasabi Dressing

Japanese salad dressings always use little or often no oil at all. They are fresh and tangy and very multi-purpose dressings that can be used on green salad, mixed vegetables or even with seafood and especially quickly seared tune.

Makes: 4-6

Total Prep Time: 5 minutes

Ingredient List:

- 1 Tbsp. of rice vinegar
- 1 Tbsp. mirin
- 1 tsp. of caster sugar
- 1 Tbsp. of dark soy sauce
- 1 tsp. of sesame oil
- 2 tsp. of wasabi paste
- 3 ½ Tbsp. of sunflower oil

zzzzzzzzzzzzzzzzzzzzzzzzzzzzzzzzzzzzzzzzzzzzzzz

Instructions:

Combine the vinegar, mirin, and sugar in a large bowl.

Stir well until all the sugar is dissolve.

Add the soy sauce, the sesame oil, and wasabi paste.

Add the sunflower oil and whisk until smooth.

22) Mints & Cottage Cheese Dressing

Avery refreshing cottage cheese dressing with mints which will delight the taste of your salad. You can always replace the cottage cheese with yogurt as well. Try to chop the mints just before you will added to the mixture; this will allow to have the full flavor of the mints in your dressing.

Makes: 4

Total Prep Time: 4 minutes

Ingredient List:

- 4 Tbsp. of cottage cheese
- 1 Tbsp. of cider vinegar
- 1 Tbsp. of mustard
- 1 tsp. of lemon juice
- 2 tsp. of fresh mints, finely chopped
- Salt and pepper

zzzzzzzzzzzzzzzzzzzzzzzzzzzzzzzzzzzzzzzzzzzzzzzz

Instructions:

Combine the cottage cheese and the mustard in a small bowl.

Whisk in the vinegar and lemon juice.

Add the fresh mints and stir well.

Season well and whisk again.

Mix the dressing to your salad and serve.

23) Lemon Vinaigrette

A very easy and quick recipe to make and this lemon vinaigrette will go perfectly well with any seafood and fish mix salad. It you find the taste too acid don't hesitate to add a tsp. of sugar.

Makes: 4

Total Prep Time: 4 minutes

Ingredient List:

- 2 Tbsp. of lemon juice
- 5 Tbsp. of olive oil
- 1 Tbsp. of chives, chopped
- 1 tsp. of warm water
- Salt and pepper

zzzzzzzzzzzzzzzzzzzzzzzzzzzzzzzzzzzzzzzzzzzzz

Instructions:

Combine a pinch of salt and the lemon juice in a small bowl.

Whisk until the salt is dissolved completely.

Add the olive oil slowly in a thin steady stream and whisk in the same time.

Add the warm water and whisk again for few second.

Add the chives and toss with the salad.

24) Mayonnaise

Mayonnaise is one of the most famous salad dressings of the world and not always easy to make it perfectly; always need some practice at first to succeed. If you want to lighten the texture just add a little water. You can also add some yogurt as well, which will make it less rich.

Makes: 4-6

Total Prep Time: 4 minutes

Ingredient List:

- 2 eggs yolk
- 2 tsp. of white vinegar
- 1 cup of sunflower oil
- 1 tsp. of Dijon mustard
- Salt and pepper

zzzzzzzzzzzzzzzzzzzzzzzzzzzzzzzzzzzzzzzzzzzzzzzzzzz

Instructions:

Place the eggs yolk and the white vinegar into a food processor or blender.

Add the mustard and season.

Process for 15 seconds or until blended.

Add the sunflower oil in a thin steady stream slowly and whisk in the same time.

Blend everything until the mixture is thick and creamy.

Adjust the flavor with more vinegar, mustard if you wish.

25) Mango & Chili Dressing

An original dressing recipe made with mango and red chili hot taste of which is to delight your salad. It is perfect as well with any grilled fish and a fennel salad or even try with some white asparagus. You can as well having the dressing without any chili.

Makes: 4-6

Total Prep Time: 8 minutes

Ingredient List:

- 1 ripe mango
- 1 red chili, seeded and chopped
- 1 Tbsp. of mustard
- 3 Tbsp. of olive oil
- 1 Tbsp. of water
- 2 drop of Tabasco
- Salt and pepper

zzzzzzzzzzzzzzzzzzzzzzzzzzzzzzzzzzzzzzzzzzzzzz

Instructions:

Extract all the flesh from the mango.

Put all the flesh into a mixer or blender.

Add the red chili and one Tbsp. of water.

Blend everything until you get a smooth purée.

Add the mustard and the Tabasco. Season.

Blend again for few second.

Add the olive oil slowly in a thin steady stream while blending in the same time.

Remove the dressing from the blender and toss the salad.

About the Author

A native of Albuquerque, New Mexico, Sophia Freeman found her calling in the culinary arts when she enrolled at the Sante Fe School of Cooking. Freeman decided to take a year after graduation and travel around Europe, sampling the cuisine from small bistros and family owned restaurants from Italy to Portugal. Her bubbly personality and inquisitive nature made her popular with the locals in the villages and when she finished her trip and came home, she had made friends for life in the places she had visited. She also came home with a deeper understanding of European cuisine.

Freeman went to work at one of Albuquerque's 5-star restaurants as a sous-chef and soon worked her way up to head chef. The restaurant began to feature Freeman's original dishes as specials on the menu and soon after, she began to write e-books with her recipes. Sophia's dishes mix local flavours with European inspiration making them irresistible to the diners in her restaurant and the online community.

Freeman's experience in Europe didn't just teach her new ways of cooking, but also unique methods of presentation. Using rich sauces, crisp vegetables and meat cooked to perfection, she creates a stunning display as well as a delectable dish. She has won many local awards for her cuisine and she continues to delight her diners with her culinary masterpieces.

Author's Afterthoughts

I want to convey my big thanks to all of my readers who have taken the time to read my book. Readers like you make my work so rewarding and I cherish each and every one of you.

Grateful cannot describe how I feel when I know that someone has chosen my work over all of the choices available online. I hope you enjoyed the book as much as I enjoyed writing it.

Feedback from my readers is how I grow and learn as a chef and an author. Please take the time to let me know your thoughts by leaving a review on Amazon so I and your fellow readers can learn from your experience.

My deepest thanks,

Sophia Freeman

https://sophia.subscribemenow.com/

Made in the USA
Monee, IL
13 April 2021